T0063336

# Speaking POSITIVE without the NEGATIVE

JUAWANNA MCGHEE

WESTBOW
PRESS
A DIVISION OF THOMAS NELSON

WestBow Press books may be ordered through booksellers or by contacting:

WestBow Press
A Division of Thomas Nelson
1663 Liberty Drive
Bloomington, IN 47403
www.westbowpress.com
1-(866) 928-1240

Scripture taken from the King James Version of the Bible.

Scripture taken from the New King James Version. Copyright 1979, 1980, 1982 by Thomas Nelson, inc. Used by permission. All rights reserved.

Scriptures taken from the Holy Bible, New International Version®, NIV®. Copyright © 1973, 1978, 1984, 2011 by Biblica, Inc.™ Used by permission of Zondervan. All rights reserved worldwide. www.zondervan.com The "NIV" and "New International Version" are trademarks registered in the United States Patent and Trademark Office by Biblica, Inc.™ All rights reserved.

ISBN: 978-1-4908-0226-8 (sc)

Library of Congress Control Number: 2013912772

Printed in the United States of America.

WestBow Press rev. date: 08/26/2013

# Contents

# Acknowledgments

To my husband, Stacy, for believing in me even when I didn't believe in myself. Thank you for encouraging me when I wanted to give up and praying for me when you saw me struggling. Without you by my side, this would have been a very hard mountain to climb. Twenty-two years together and looking forward to spending the rest of my life with you. I love you so much.

To my Children and my Grandchildren

I would like to say thank you for just being my children. We have had our difficult times but the love we have can conquer anything. I wouldn't trade it for nothing in the world. I pray that you all are successful in whatever your hearts desire and I also pray that God is always first in your lives.

To my parents, for being there for us when times got rough.

To Pastor Erven A. and First Lady Kimble for loving my family. Thank you for your words of wisdom and for keeping your hands outstretched toward us.

# Dedication

THIS BOOK IS dedicated to my son, Dallas. All the late nights we sat up talking about those things that were bothering you. How you were trying so hard to make a change in your life but it just wasn't working. Your little notes you would write to me, waking me up at midnight because you needed to talk (knowing I had to go to work that next morning). I got up and listened because I needed to encourage you so you would know that God was right there. As I ministered to you, I was ministering to myself because I needed to know God was right there too.

# Foreword

FAITH COMES BY hearing, and hearing by the word of God. If only we could grab hold of those words. In order to have faith and have it grow, you have to hear God's word. There must be a constant intake to handle the demands of life. Oftentimes I've found myself burdened by trials and instead of drawing closer to the Lord I pulled away, leaving myself vulnerable to the enemy's attack. I'd always view the situation from the negative perspective and not the positive - it was always what I couldn't do or what wouldn't happen. Sadly, I would have been one of the naysayers in the crowd when Caleb told the children of Israel that they were well able to overcome and possess the Promised Land. I would have been one of the doubters but I soon learned that doubters never advance. They talk about moving forward but walk the same path over and over (sometimes for 40 years). I was tired of the same old routine and results and that is why I can completely identify with the message of this book: To speak the positive without the negative; to focus on God's promises instead of your circumstances.

If you long to live in a new spiritual stage of your life, if you want to step out of that powerless routine and walk in the power of God, this book is for you. To my dear friend Juawanna, you've got a winner here.

Michael Seay, Pastor
St. Luke, Bonita, Louisiana
Michael Seay, Author, Director
Restoring the Glory
24 Hours Till Jesus Comes
Heaven's Glory Ministries (Director)

# Introduction

I N OUR SOCIETY today, we are faced with so many different issues. We have peer pressure, financial difficulties, and different kinds of abuse: sexual, verbal, physical and mental. One of our biggest problems today is negativity. There are so many negative influences before us. We have the television, radio and computers and each one gives out plenty of negative messages. The only way we are going to ever be able to stand in this negative world is to trust God and trust Him only. Life and death is in the power of the tongue. We can speak life into our lives and our situations or we can speak death. One of the reasons why things don't go the way they should is because we don't pay attention to some of the things we say. Example: I want to become a gospel-recording artist, but I know it can't happen for me. The positive was spoken and then there came the negative. If we allow doubt to take over us, we are sure to fail. Doubting is a sin and it will cause us to second guess everything, even our instructions from God. When we start to second-guess, we open the door for the enemy to come in. Speaking of opening the door to the enemy: When God gives us instructions, we can't be so quick to tell everyone. Everyone is not going to be happy for you and everyone will not understand God's will for your life. There are people who think they know what's best for you but believe me, they don't and there are people who just want you to fail. One thing I found out is that you can not please man: No matter how hard you try. So therefore, we have to stay strong in the Lord and put on the whole armour of God.

Finally my brethren, be strong in the Lord, and in the power of His might. Put on the whole armour of God that you may be able to stand against the wiles of the devil. For we do not wrestle against flesh and blood, but against principalities, against powers, against the rulers of the darkness of this age, against spiritual hosts of wickedness in the heavenly places. Therefore take up the whole armor of God, that you may be able to withstand in the evil day, and having done all, to stand. Stand therefore, having girded your waist with truth, having put on the breastplate of righteousness; And having shod your feet with the preparation of the gospel of peace; Above all, taking the shield of Faith, with which you will be able to quench all the fiery darts of the wicked one. And take the helmet of salvation, and the sword of the Spirit, which is the word of God: Praying always with all prayer and supplication in the Spirit, being watchful to this end with all perseverance and supplication for all the saints. (Ephesians 6:10 -18 NKJV) We are God's people and we have been called to do God's will. This is why our walk and our talk has to be spoken in the same language so that we may be successful in whatever God is calling us to do. We can not speak one thing and do another. Our actions have to line up with our words and our actions and words has to line up with God's will. Putting our trust in the Lord is a sure pathway to eternal life, prosperity, peace and joy (everything that is positive). In this book, you will read about many different things that cause us to speak negative and we will find out why it is so important for us to become a positive people.

## The Right Attitude

We have to know that our attitudes play a very important role in being able to speak positive words into our situations. Our attitudes can hinder the blessings God has for us, because we let our circumstances get the best of us. We can't let our circumstances control our attitudes. We have to have control over our attitudes to be able to stand in the midst of our circumstances. Now, there is only one way we can have control of our attitudes and that is if God is in complete control of us. God has to have a permanent place of residency in our hearts, because our hearts can be very wicked. Brood of vipers! How can you being evil, speak good things? For out of the abundance of the heart the mouth speaks. (Matthew 12:34 NKJV) We have to be very careful how we react to things, because our attitudes can make us or they can break us.

## Letting Our Attitude Make Us

We have to be determined that no matter what comes our way, we will keep a positive attitude. God says in Hebrews 13:5 (NKJV) Let your conduct be without covetousness; be content with such things as you have: for He Himself has said, I will never leave you nor forsake you. There is nothing that comes our way that God does not know about. If we decide to let our attitudes make us, the process of getting where we want to be (as long as where we want to be lines up with God's will for us) will be a lot smoother and faster. I am not saying that, because we have a positive attitude things won't happen. I am saying that when those things happen, our positive attitudes will help us overcome our obstacles. Having a positive attitude is Christ-like. Our Lord and Savior Jesus Christ is a perfect example of having a positive attitude.

Jesus Christ, the One who committed no sin, suffered a great deal: He was beaten and spit on. He never lied yet He was accused of it, but since He knew the truth His attitude never changed. He knew who He was and what He was here to do. We must know who we are and whose we are to be able to hear from God to know what we are suppose to do.

What we deal with on a day to day basis and the things that we go through could never compare to what Jesus Christ our Lord and Savior went through the last few hours that He spent on earth before dying on the Cross. So we should let our positive attitudes so shine forth from this day forward. If Christ could endure the pain and suffering that He went through, I know we can deal with our issues because God says in 1 Corinthians 10:13 (NKJV) No temptation has overtaken you except such as is common to man; but God is faithful, who will not allow you to be tempted beyond what you are able, but with the temptation will also make the way of escape, that you may be able to bear it. So, the next time you are tempted to be negative remember there is a way to escape it. (Through Christ)

## Letting Our Attitude Break Us

One of the easiest things to do is "**miss the mark**". Having a negative attitude will always cause us to miss the mark. Negative thinking is not Christ-like. Having a negative attitude takes away our joy, our peace, our strength and it takes away from our families. Holding on to a negative attitude will cost us time that we can't afford to lose. Having a negative attitude causes sickness, depression, low self-esteem, discouragement and sleepless nights. Have you ever been around someone that always has something negative to say? (Not good company) Some people have lost good friends because they were so negative and some have lost good jobs. The enemy loves negative people. A negative person can not encourage anyone because negative words tear down, not build up. If we take the time to look back over the years, we will see that nothing good has ever come out of being negative.

I want you to take a few minutes and think about something negative you may have said to someone or something negative that was said to you. How did it make you feel? Negative words can leave lasting scars. Always think before you speak. That was a lesson I had to learn.

# ✛ Notes ▬

_____

_____

_____

_____

_____

_____

_____

_____

_____

_____

_____

_____

_____

_____

_____

_____

_____

_____

_____

_____

_____

_____

_____

_____

# My Prayer Life

PRAYER IS A very important part of our Christian journey. Prayer is our way of communicating with God. By praying, it shows that we need and depend on God. OUR PRAYERS CAN NOT BE REPLACED BY OUR WORKS. By praying, it allows us to become more in tune with God and it makes it easier to recognize God's voice when He is speaking to us. God is not the only one who wants to communicate with us, that is why it is so important that we pray at all times. The enemy is at all times ready to seek, steal and destroy. If we are not praying like we should, the enemy will try to find a way to bring destruction in our lives. Our relationship with God is the only thing that will keep us and prayer is the Key. As the older generation would say "just a little talk with Jesus would make everything alright." I finally understood that saying. There have been times when I didn't know which way to go or what to do. I was confused about everything but my talk with Jesus made everything alright. No, my situation did not change at that moment, but just being in God's presence brought about a change in me. I was no longer confused because I found peace in the midst of my situation.

Pray without ceasing. In everything give thanks: for this is the will of God in Christ Jesus for you. Do not quench the Spirit. Do not despise prophecies. Test all things; hold fast what is good. Abstain from every form of evil. Now may the God of peace Himself sanctify you completely; and may your whole spirit, soul and body be preserved blameless at the coming of our Lord Jesus Christ. (1 Thessalonians 5:17-23 NKJV)

In this chapter, we will talk about the different but very important aspects of prayer and how they play a very important role in our positive speaking.

## Faith

Faith is a belief in or confident attitude toward God. Praying in faith is having confidence in God and not in ourselves, believing that He is the only true and living God. When praying in faith, there can't be any room for doubt.

### James 1:5-8 (NKJV)

If any of you lacks wisdom, let him ask of God, who gives to all liberally and without reproach, and it will be given to him. But let him ask in faith, with no doubting, for he who doubts is like a wave of the sea driven and tossed by the wind. For let

not that man suppose that he will receive anything from the
Lord, he is a double-minded man, unstable in all his ways.

### Matthew 17:20-21 (NKJV)
So Jesus said to them, "Because of your unbelief; for assuredly,
I say to you, if you have faith as a mustard seed, you will
say to this mountain, Move from here to there, and it will
move; and nothing will be impossible for you. However,
this kind does not go out except by prayer and fasting."

### Matthew 21:21-22 (NKJV)
So Jesus answered and said to them, Assuredly, I say to you, If
you have faith, and do not doubt, you will not only do what
was done to the fig tree, but also if you say to this mountain,
Be removed and be cast into the sea; it will be done. And
whatever things, you ask in prayer, believing, you will receive.

# Worship

Worship is reverent devotion and allegiance pledged to God.
Worship is our way of showing that only God is deserving
of our highest praise and respect. There is nothing that we
can do or say that will ever compare to God.

### Psalm 96:9 (NKJV)
Oh, worship the Lord in the beauty of holiness!
Tremble before Him, all the earth.

### Psalm 95:6 (NKJV)
Oh come, let us worship and bow down; Let
us kneel before the Lord our Maker.

### Psalm 99:5 (NKJV)
Exalt the Lord our God, And worship at
His footstool- for He is holy.

# Confession

Confession is an admission of sins. Prayer causes us to draw closer to God and being closer to God causes us to be mindful of the things we do and say. Now, being mindful of those things should cause us to want to confess our sins when we know that we have sinned and fallen short. We should also ask God to show us those sins that were committed unknowingly as well because so many of us do and say things and we do not realize that we have sinned.

*Proverbs 14:12 (NKJV)*
There is a way that seems right to a man,
But its end is the way of death.

*Psalm 32:5 (NKJV)*
I acknowledge my sin to You, And my iniquity I have not hidden. I said, I will confess my transgressions to the Lord; and You forgave the iniquity of my sin.

*1 John:9 (NKJV)*
If we confess our sins, He is faithful and just to forgive us our sins and to cleanse us from all unrighteousness.

# Adoration

Adoration is the act of worship, of paying honor, giving reverence and being obedient to God. Adoration is our way of expressing our love toward God. God showed His love toward us when He sent His son to die for our sins. Can you think of a greater love?

*John 3:16 (NKJV)*
For God so loved the world that He gave His
only begotten Son, that whoever believes in Him
should not perish but have everlasting life.

# Thanksgiving

Thanksgiving is the aspect of praise that gives thanks to God for what He does for us. To be able to be thankful you have to be grateful. We should be thankful because God has given us grace and mercy and He has not giving us what we truly deserve. Are you grateful for where you are at this moment in your life because things could be so much worse. Can you look back and say God has brought you a mighty long way (with a smile)? Did you thank Him for the sins that He brought you out of? Did you thank Him for not letting you die while you were caught up in your sins? Did you thank Him for not turning His back on you even though you turned yours on Him? (Unconditional Love) We all have so much to be thankful for. God has been and always will be so good to us; no matter where we are in our lives.

# God's Riches At Christ's Expense

*Psalm 50:14 (NKJV)*
Offer to God thanksgiving, And pay your vows to the Most High.

*Psalm 116:17 (NKJV)*
I will offer to You the sacrifice of thanksgiving,
And will call upon the name of the Lord.

*Psalm 100:4 (NKJV)*
Enter into His gates with thanksgiving, And into His courts
with praise. Be thankful to Him, and bless His name.

# Praise

Praise is an act of worship or acknowledgement by which
the virtues of deeds of another are recognized and extolled.
Faith, worship, confession and adoration equals praise.
Praise is speaking well of Him that we highly esteem and
love more than anything; whose name is God.

*Psalms 63:3 (NKJV)*
Because your lovingkindness is better than
life, My lips shall praise you.

*Psalms 145:3 (NKJV)*
Great is the Lord, and greatly to be praised;
And His greatness is unsearchable.

*Psalms 150:1-6 (NKJV)*
Praise the Lord! Praise God in His sanctuary; Praise Him
in His mighty firmament! Praise Him for His mighty acts;
Praise Him according to His excellent greatness! Praise Him
with the sound of the trumpet; Praise Him with the lute
and harp! Praise Him with the timbrel and dance; Praise
Him with stringed instruments and flutes! Praise Him
with loud cymbals; Praise Him with clashing cymbals! Let
everything that has breath praise the Lord. Praise the Lord!

# Watch What You Say
## Prayer has power over everything.

James 5:16b (NKJV) The effective fervent prayer of a righteous man avails much.

When we go to God in prayer, we are not going to impress God with fancy words. (Big words we can't pronounce correctly and don't know the meaning of). God desires a humble spirit. He knows what's in your heart even if you can't say a word.

### Matthew 6: 5-8 (NKJV)
And when you pray, you shall not be like the hypocrites. For they love to pray standing in the synagogues and on the corners of the streets, that they may be seen by men. Assuredly, I say to you, they have their reward. But you, when you pray, go into your room, and when you have shut the door, pray to your Father who is in the secret place; and your Father who sees in secret will reward you openly. And when you pray, do not use vain repetitions as the heathen do. For they think that they will be heard for their many words. Therefore do not be like them. For your Father knows the things you have need of before you ask Him.

Take a few minutes and write down the things that you are thankful for.

# Notes

# Forgiving

W E, BEING GOD's people, have to learn to be forgiving. Forgiveness is an act of excusing or pardoning others in spite of their slights, short comings and errors. Holding on to unforgiveness can lead to major health problems. Unforgiveness is a sin (poison) and sin brings about sickness and some sicknesses can lead to death.

Stress, heart problems, headaches and stomach problems can all be associated with unforgiveness. Every problem that is named can cause death. **Stress** can cause a stroke, which can lead to death.

**Heart Problems** can cause a heart attack, which can lead to death.

**Headaches** can cause an aneurysm, which can lead to death.

**Stomach Problems** can cause eating disorders, which can lead to lack of food and eventually cause death.

Forgiving is a heart issue. It works from the inside out. You can say you have forgiven someone all day long but if your heart is not in it then your actions will eventually prove that you did not mean what you said (If you don't mean it in your heart, your actions will eventually line up with your heart but if you mean it from your heart then your actions will line up with your heart.) **Did you get that? Like I said "forgiving is a heart issue".**

## Why Is It So Hard To Forgive?

Fear (among other things) has a lot to do with us not wanting to forgive. We fear that if we forgive others they will do it again. Probably so, but God tells us in His word that we are to forgive. Another reason is because what they've done hurts too much and you feel like they don't deserve to be forgiven (they deserve punishment) but God says in:

*Roman 12:19 (NKJV)*
Beloved, do not avenge yourselves, but rather give place to wrath; for it is written, Vengeance is mine, I will repay, "says the Lord.

The most important reason of all (we think) is because we feel like we have forgiven them too many times and we want to know why do we have to keep forgiving them, but Peter already beat us to the question.

*Matthew 18:21-22: (NKJV)*
Then Peter came to Him and said, Lord, how often shall my brother sin against me, and I forgive him? Up to seven times? Jesus said to him, I do not say to you, Up to seven times, but up to seventy times seven.

You won't be able to keep up with the count, so stop counting and keep forgiving.

*Matthew 5:43-45 (NKJV)*
You have heard that it was said, "You shall love your neighbor and hate your enemy. But I say to you, love your enemies, bless those who curse you, do good to those that hate you and pray for those who spitefully use you and persecute you, that you may be sons of your Father in heaven: for He makes His sun rise on the evil and on the good, and sends rain on the just and on the unjust.

Another reason why we don't forgive is because we don't have a clean heart. Our hearts are filled with anger, hatred, disappointment, hurt, jealousy and envy. God does not dwell in an unclean heart. Where there is Love, there is God. We have to forgive in order to be forgiven.

*Matthew 6:12-15 says: (NKJV)*
And forgive us our debts, as we forgive our debtors. And do not lead us into temptation, But deliver us from the evil one. For Yours is the kingdom and the power and the glory forever. Amen. For if you forgive men their trespasses, your heavenly Father will also forgive you. But if you do not forgive men their trespasses, neither will your Father forgive your trespasses.

We need to pray and ask God to cleanse our hearts and give us a right Spirit so that He may dwell in our hearts.

*Psalm 51:10 (NKJV)*
Create in me a clean heart, O God, And renew a steadfast spirit within me.

# Where Is My Peace?

The definition for peace is a state of calm and quiet; freedom from disturbing thoughts or emotions. When you choose not to forgive, you can't truly experience this freedom. Peace only comes from God and to get that peace you have to have a close relationship with God. Holding on to unforgiveness is a waste of our precious time and energy. When you choose not to forgive you give control to the person or persons that you feel have wronged you. If God is in complete control of our lives then no one else can be in control. I am a true example of an unforgiving person. There was not a three strikes you're out with me, it was, you hurt me one time and it was over. You did not talk or speak to me, you did not come around me, it was over. You had your chance, you blew it. All of that happened because I didn't have a relationship with God. When I started going to Bible study, reading God's word and praying with a sincere heart, I had a life-changing experience. **God Changed Me!!** God knew my heart was not clean and I knew it wasn't clean. I had to be honest with God, confess those things and ask God to change my heart. He already knew what was in my heart, He was just waiting on me to finally see it for myself and come to Him for help. Just like He is waiting on you. I thank God for the change that He brought about in me. When there has been a change in you, there is no way that you can continue to hold on to unforgiveness. Choosing to forgive can bring about healing and peace of mind.

*Ephesians 4:32 (NKJV)*
And be kind to one another, tenderhearted, forgiving
one another, even as God in Christ forgave you.

*Philippians 4:7 (NKJV) says:*
And the peace of God, which surpasses all understanding,
will guard your hearts and minds through Christ Jesus.

*Colossians 3:12-15 (NKJV)*
Therefore, as the elect of God, holy and beloved, put on tender
mercies, kindness, humility, meekness, longsuffering; bearing
with one another, and forgiving one another, if anyone has a
complaint against another: even as Christ forgave you, so you
also must do. But above all these things put on love, which is the
bond of perfection. And let the peace of God rule in your hearts,
to which also you were called in one body; and be thankful.

*Romans 12:20-21 (NKJV)*
Therefore "If your enemy is hungry, feed him; If he is thirsty,
give him a drink; For in so doing you will heap coals of fire
on his head." Do not be overcome by evil, but overcome
evil with good. This is where you will find your peace!

Take a few minutes and write down the names of the
people that you know you haven't truly forgiven. Please be
honest with yourself and God because He already knows.
Guess what. I just thought of someone that I hadn't forgiven.
I thought I just had anger toward the person and didn't want
to be in their presence. Thank you Jesus for showing me
that that is unforgiveness. That burden was lifted as I just
forgave that person. I'm free and you will be free as well.
Start Forgiving.

# ✦ Notes ⸺

# Tithing

Tithing is one of the most important parts of our spiritual walk and growth. Becoming a cheerful tither is a choice and an act of obedience to God. When we don't tithe, we are not only hurting the church, we are hurting ourselves, our families and our finances.

Malachi 3:8-9 (NKJV) says "Will a man rob God? Yet you have robbed Me. "But you say, 'In what way have we robbed You?' "In tithes and offerings. ⁹ You are cursed with a curse, For you have robbed Me, Even this whole nation.

Tithing is to comprehend and respond to the word of God by giving ten percent of your first fruit. Take a second and think about something: Would you want someone to give to you, what already belongs to you with the wrong attitude? Ex: I give a friend $50 for a bill and she is suppose to give it back on payday but she gives it back grudgingly and with anger. The money belongs to me, why would she give me my money with that attitude? Well, that's the same way God feels about us giving Him what already belongs to Him. We can not give to God grudgingly. When we come to a realization that nothing belongs to us, we will be able to give cheerfully and abundantly.

Proverbs 3:9-10 (NKJV): Honor the Lord with your possessions, And with the firstfruits of all your increase: So your barns will be filled with plenty, and your vats will overflow with new wine.

## The Purpose For Tithing

Our purpose for tithing is to become obedient unto God for this is right. (Deuteronomy 6:18 (NKJV) And you shall do what is right and good in the sight of the Lord: that it may be well with you, and that you may go in and possess the good land which the Lord swore to your fathers.) In doing this, we are being obedient to what God has called us to do.

We all have things that come our way when we want to become faithful tithers because God allows circumstances to come about to test our faith. (bills) Giving of our tithes is a very important part of our walk with Christ. Malachi 3:10-11 (NKJV) says: Bring all the tithes into the storehouse, That there may be food in My house, and try Me now in this, Says the Lord of hosts, If I will not open for you the windows of heaven And pour out for you such blessing that there will not be room enough to receive it. And I will rebuke the devourer for your sakes, So that he will not destroy the fruit of your ground; Nor shall the vine fail to bear fruit for you in the field, Says the Lord of hosts. God also said in 2 Corinthians 9:6 (NKJV): ⁶But this I say: He who sows sparingly will also reap sparingly, and he who sows bountifully will also reap bountifully. We know that it is always better to give than it is to receive. If we want the best, we have to give our best. One thing is for sure; we can't beat God giving.

*Psalms 24:1 (NKJV)*
The earth is the Lord's and all its fullness; The
world and those who dwell therein.

## What Is Tithing?

Tithing is the practice of giving a tenth of one's income or property as an offering to God. Tithing is not only about money, because God has given us more than money. He has given us: **Time and Talents** as well as **Treasures.** We can spend time encouraging others, helping the poor, volunteering, coming up with fun and exciting ways to spread the Good News about God in our neighborhoods and our communities. I know that we have so little time on our hands these days with work, school work and activities, cooking dinner and trying to take care of everyone's need. If we would just make time for God, HOW GREAT IS THE REWARD. Using our talents is another form of tithing. We all have different talents: singing, dancing, miming, typing, sorting, making copies, etc. Even the smallest thing that we consider not to be of any value is of great value in furthering the Kingdom of Heaven. God does not consider anything of no use (when it helps to build up and not tear down). God does not consider one to be greater than the other.

Our treasure is very important. Our money helps to keep the lights on, water and gas paid and the phones on. All of which we need to keep the church functioning. The church staff has to be paid for their jobs, especially our pastor for this is his job.

## True Prosperity

You might say, what about those that don't believe in God? Why do they prosper and why does it seem like they get everything that they want. We have to know that everything that looks good to us is not always good for us. Matthew 6:19-21 (NKJV) Do not lay up for yourselves treasures on earth, where moth and rust destroy and where thieves break in and steal; but lay up for yourselves treasures in heaven, where neither moth nor rust destroys, and where thieves do not break in and steal: For where your treasure is, there your heart will be also.

We have to seek the true prosperity of God. True prosperity is not having millions of dollars, big homes and nice cars. It's trusting God to provide for us daily.

*Matthew 6: 31 -32 (NKJV)*
Therefore do not worry saying, "What shall we eat?"
or "What shall we drink?" or "What shall we wear?"
For after all these things the Gentiles seek. For your
heavenly Father knows that you need all these things.

*Matthew 6:24 (NKJV)*
No one can serve two masters: for either he will hate the one,
and love the other; or else he will be loyal to the one and
despise the other. You cannot serve God and mammon.

1 Timothy 6:10a (NKJV) For the love of money is a
root of all kinds of evil. True prosperity does not come from
having worldly possessions; rather it is the heavenly wisdom
and spiritual knowledge that comes only from God.

*Matthew 6:33 (NKJV)*
But seek first the kingdom of God and His righteousness,
and all these things shall be added to you

God desires for His children to be prosperous, but those
things of the world should not be our definition of prosperity.

*Matthew 19:23-24 (NKJV)*
Then Jesus said to His disciples, Assuredly, I say to you that
it is hard for a rich man to enter the kingdom of heaven. And
again I say to you, it is easier for a camel to go through the eye
of a needle, than for a rich man to enter the kingdom of God

When you link prosperity to God and prosperity to
the world, there is a difference. Prosperity from God is
everlasting and prosperity of the world is temporary.

*1 Timothy 6:17-19 (NKJV)*
Command those who are rich in this present age not to be haughty,
nor to trust in uncertain riches but in the living God, who gives us
richly all things to enjoy; Let them do good, that they be rich in good
works, ready to give, willing to share; storing up for themselves a good
foundation for the time to come, that they may lay hold on eternal life.

# ✛ Notes ➝

_____

_____

_____

_____

_____

_____

_____

_____

_____

_____

_____

_____

_____

_____

_____

_____

_____

_____

_____

_____

_____

_____

_____

_____

# Letting Go of the Past

ONE OF THE most common reasons why we can't move forward is because we never stop looking backwards. We have to let go of the past. The past is just what it is "the past." The past means time gone by; something that happened or was done in a former time. There are so many of us who keep holding on to the past because we haven't forgiven ourselves or someone for some of the things that has happened in our lives. There is strength in our God. God is our comforter and He will give us all the strength that we need to keep looking ahead.

*Psalm18:2 (NKJV):*
The Lord is my rock and my fortress and my deliverer;
My God, my strength in whom I will trust; My shield
and the horn of my salvation, my stronghold.

Another reason why it is so hard to let go of the past is because we are not happy with ourselves, so we find ourselves trying to be someone else or something that we are not. God has made us all unique so there is no way we can be no one but ourselves. There is no way around it. Trying to be someone else can only lead to disappointment and hurt to us and to the one's that truly loves us for who we are. If we are not being ourselves, we will not be able to function in the areas God will have us to (effectively). When God created us, He was pleased.

*Genesis 1:31a (NKJV)*
Then God saw everything that He had
made, and indeed it was very good.

If God is pleased with us, why can't we be pleased with ourselves. We are beautiful because we are made in God's image and He makes no mistakes. If we are not pleased with ourselves, we might as well say "God, you messed up". We have to be pleased with ourselves in order to have joy in our lives. If we don't have joy, no one around us will have joy.

JUST LET ME BE ME
THE ONE GOD INTENDED
FOR ME TO BE

# I Did It! It's Done! Let It Go!

We have to have the right state of mind when dealing with our past. The right state of mind is a Christ-like mind. We have to think like Christ. Christ never held anything against us when He went to the cross, in fact, He prayed for us. He prayed for those who crucified Him and He asked His Father to forgive them for they knew not what they did. Those people were lost and so were we. If we knew who Christ truly was, there are so many things we would have done differently. We live and we learn. Now if Jesus Christ, being who He is, can forgive us for our past then why can't we forgive ourselves? The time has come for us to let it go.

*Psalm 51:1-4a (NKJV)*
Have mercy upon me, O God. According to Your lovingkindness; According to the multitude of Your tender mercies; Blot out my transgressions; Wash me thoroughly from my iniquity, And cleanse me from my sin. For I acknowledge my transgressions, and my sin is always before me. Against You, You only, have I sinned, And done this evil in Your sight

## But You Don't Know What I've Done

And you don't know what I've done. Your sin is no greater than mine or anyone else. We all have sinned and fallen short of God's Glory. For all have sinned and fall short of the glory of God (Romans 3:23 NKJV). But His grace and mercy is sufficient for all of us. God loves us despite all that we have done. The enemy loves to keep bringing up our past. If he knows that our past always seem to make us lose focus, that's what he will use. We have to find our strength in Jesus and resist the devil and he will flee (James 4:7 NKJV Therefore submit to God. Resist the devil and he will flee from you). Nothing and no one can stand up against the power of Jesus Christ. Do you know who you are? But you are a chosen generation, a royal priesthood, a holy nation, His own special people; that you may proclaim the praises of Him who called you out of darkness into His marvelous light (1 Peter 2:9 NKJV) We are special in the sight of God. What makes us so special is the fact that He chose us. How awesome it is to be chosen by the One that created heaven and earth.

## Does God Still Love Me?

God never stopped loving you and He never will. John 3:16 (NKJV) says for God so loved the world that He gave His only begotten Son that whoever believes in Him should not perish, but have everlasting life. Just like a parent never stops loving their children no matter how angry they get at them and no matter what the child has done. We want the best for our children, we don't want anything bad to happen to them and we will do any and everything possible to protect them. That's how God feels about us: He wants the best for us, He doesn't want anything bad to happen to us and He will protect us. And just like our children we have to suffer the consequences for our actions. Just like our children have to be disciplined, so do we. We discipline our children because we love them and the punishment will cause them to do better and to be a better person. Well, God disciplines us for that same reason. So, no matter what we have done in the past, God still loves us and He has forgiven us for our past. There is no greater Love than the Love God has for us.

*Romans 8:38 - 39 (NKJV)*
For I am persuaded that neither death nor life, nor angels nor principalities nor powers, nor things present nor things to come, nor height nor depth, nor any other created thing, shall be able to separate us from the love of God which is in Christ Jesus our Lord.

Are you ready for take off? Is there anything in your past that you haven't let go of? Write it down and tell God that it is what's keeping you from moving ahead. Just know that once you give this to God things are going to start happening. Get ready and enjoy the ride.

# ✛ Notes ━

# YOU

# ARE

# BEAUTIFUL

# Excuses, Excuses

HAVE YOU EVER noticed that we have an excuse for everything that we choose not to do? The reason I used the word "choose" is because we have a choice to do right or to do wrong. We also have a choice whether or not we will follow God's commandments. If we choose to keep God's commandments He promised us that we would have a long life with peace. (Proverbs 3:1-2 (NKJV) My son, do not forget my law; But let your heart keep my commands: For length of days and long life And peace, they will add to you.)

There is a word that can describe someone who is always making excuses for their actions. It is called "Selfish". We can be very selfish and not even realize it. The reason why we sometimes don't realize it is because we are always caught up in "I". If "I" did something and "I" don't get recognition for it, then "I" have issues. It is not about "I". Everything we do is for our Lord and if we trusted in the Lord, we would not have to make excuses because we would know that as long as God is in control then anything that "I" do is not about me. Proverb 3:5-6 (NKJV)

Trust in the Lord with all your heart; and lean not on your own understanding. In all your ways acknowledge Him, And He shall direct your paths.

It is easy to make excuses for not doing the things God has told us to do. Jeremiah made an excuse: Then said I, Ah, Lord God! Behold, I cannot speak: for I am a youth. (Jeremiah 1:6 NKJV) But God did not settle for his excuse and He replied "Do not say, I am a youth: For you shall go to all to whom I send you, and whatever I command you, you shall speak. Do not be afraid of their faces: For I am with you to deliver you, says the Lord. (Jeremiah 1:7-8 NKJV) A lot of us feel like Jeremiah did. We think we are to young or not equipped for the task at hand but God says otherwise.

### Jeremiah 1:5 (NKJV)
Before I formed you in the womb I knew you; Before you were born I sanctified you: I ordained you a prophet to the nations."

So, therefore, we do not have any excuse for not doing the will of God because He said that He knew use before we were formed.

### Jeremiah 1:9b-10 (NKJV)
Behold, I have put My words in your mouth. See, I have this day set you over the nations and over the kingdoms, To root out and to pull down, To destroy and to throw down, To build and to plant."

Jonah came up with one: God told Jonah to go to Nineveh, and cry out against it; because their wickedness had come up before God. Jonah decided he was going to leave the presence of God because he didn't want to do what God had commanded him to do. God did not settle for what Jonah did so He caused Jonah to be swallowed by a fish.

Now the Lord had prepared a great fish to swallow Jonah. And Jonah was in the belly of the fish three days and three nights. Jonah 1:17 (NKJV)

Jonah didn't want to do it because he knew God was a forgiving God and he didn't want God to forgive the people. Jonah's reason was very different from Jeremiah's. Jeremiah was afraid and Jonah was being disobedient. Jonah knew God's heart and he knew if he cried out for the people God would forgive them. Jonah 4:1-2 (NKJV)

But it displeased Jonah exceedingly, and he became angry. So he prayed to the Lord, and said, "Ah, Lord, was not this what I said when I was still in my country? Therefore I fled previously to Tarshish; for I know that You are a gracious and merciful God, slow to anger and abundant in lovingkindness, One who relents from doing harm.

Wow! That sounds so familiar and so selfish and just like Jonah, we can cause the people around us to suffer by being disobedient. When Jonah decided to be disobedient and got on that boat, everyone on the boat had to go through the storm. Can you think of a time when you were disobedient and the people around you had to suffer because of it? Have you ever not wanted to pray for someone because you felt like they were going to be forgiven? Or have you ever gotten angry because someone didn't get the punishment you thought they deserved?

*Jonah 4:4 (NKJV)*
Then the Lord said, "Is it right for you to be angry?"

*I ask the same question. Is it right that we be angry?*

Moses even had a few: Moses seemed to have forgotten who he was in the Lord's sight so he asked God: Who am I that I should go to Pharaoh, and that I should bring the children of Israel out of Egypt? Exodus 3:11 (NKJV) Moses came up with many more excuses. He said that he needed to know what to tell the people if they asked who sent him and he even started to complain about the way he spoke.

*Exodus 3:13 (NKJV)*
Then Moses said to God, "Indeed, when I come to the children of Israel and say to them, 'The God of your fathers has sent me to you,' and they say to me, 'What is His name?' what shall I say to them?"

Exodus 4:10 (NKJV) Then Moses said to the Lord, O my Lord, I am not eloquent, neither before nor since You have spoken to Your servant: but I am slow of speech, and slow of tongue.

God had an answer for every excuse Moses came up with but eventually God became angry with Moses. (Exodus 4-14 NKJV)

*Exodus 3:14-15a (NKJV)*
And God said to Moses, "I AM WHO I AM." And He said, "Thus
you shall say to the children of Israel, 'I AM has sent me to you.'
Moreover God said to Moses, Thus you shall say to the children
of Israel: 'The Lord God of your fathers, the God of Abraham,
the God of Isaac, and the God of Jacob, has sent me to you.

*Exodus 4:11-12 (NKJV)*
So the Lord said to him, "Who has made man's mouth?
Or who makes the mute, the deaf, the seeing, or the blind?
Have not I, the Lord? Now therefore, go, and I will be
with your mouth and teach you what you shall say."

Sometimes we come up with excuses because just like
Jeremiah, we don't think we are ready or think we are too
young: like Jonah, we are disobedient (selfish) and don't
want God to forgive others because they have done wrong,
or like Moses, we forget who we are. We have to remember
that if God has told us to do something, He has already
equipped us to do it because God does not desire for any of
His people to perish.

What if God had come up with an excuse not to send
His Son to the cross to die for our sins? God does not need
us to do anything. He has all power in His hand. He calls
us to do His will in order for us to glorify Him.

## Stop Worrying About Your Neighbor

A lot of us determine what we do by what someone else does.
We say "why do I have to do this, so and so didn't have to
do it". We will be held accountable for our own actions. So

and so can not get us into heaven. Worrying about what the other person is doing only causes us to miss out on what God has planned for us. If we had the "Just Do It" attitude we could be successful in every area of our lives. Doors will open that no man can close. God says he will supply every one of our needs.

Philippians 4:19 (NKJV) says "And my God shall supply all your need according to His riches in glory by Christ Jesus."

If our eyes were stayed on God, we would do what we know to do and not worry about what our neighbor is doing. God is our Director, our neighbor is not. When God called Abraham to sacrifice his son, He did not say "Abraham, you and your neighbor go and sacrifice your son".

We often live our lives based on what other people think. Some of the decisions that we make are centered around someone else's opinion. We have to start living a life that is pleasing unto God and not unto man.

*Psalm 118:8 (NKJV)*
It is better to trust in the Lord than to put confidence in man.

# ✦ What's on your mind? ✦

---

---

---

---

---

---

---

---

---

---

---

---

---

---

---

---

---

---

---

---

---

# It Was Meant For Bad

MY FAMILY AND I were involved in a 40 day fast along with my church family. We knew things were going to happen because when you have decided that you are going to make a sacrifice unto the Lord, the enemy gets angry. My husband was in car accident and our truck was totaled and one day during the fast the enemy tried to tear my home apart. My kids were fighting each other, my husband was angry because of it and my home had a heaviness that I could feel every time I walked through the door. I did not like the way it felt so I told my kids and my husband that our home was a place where God has to dwell and we were going to get it right. Everyone was in their own mood and did not want to apologize. I decided to talk to each one of them separately and I had to remind them that they had to apologize and forgive in order to be forgiven for their own actions. Matthew 6:14-15 (NKJV) says for if you forgive men their trespasses, your heavenly Father will also forgive you. But if you do not forgive men their trespasses, neither will your Father forgive your trespasses.

## The "Reminder"

Sometimes we have to be reminded of the things we did in order for us to see clearly. When I was talking to my daughter, she kept bringing up reasons why she didn't want to apologize and forgive. I let her give me every reason she could think of and then I reminded her of some of the things that she had done and said to hurt others and how she was apologized to and forgiven for. My daughter had come to the conclusion that she was just going to pack up and leave. I told her that, if that's what she wanted to do it was okay, but she still had to apologize and forgive if she wanted God to forgive her and she wanted to be blessed. I also explained to her how important it was for her to do it as soon as possible. Ephesians 4:26-27 (NKJV) Be angry, and do not sin, do not let the sun go down on your wrath, nor give place to the devil.

It is so important for us to forgive one another when we hurt each other. Eventually, after being reminded of the things she had been forgiven for, she broke down in tears. I felt God moving in our home. I had already had a conversation with my husband and my son and all was well with them, but I knew she would be the hardest to break. God is so awesome, He went before me and broke down the wall that she had started to build up. We need God to be a part of every area of our lives.

## After The Storm

Later in the day, I took my son with me to run errands, just to give them some time apart. I talked a little more to him about forgiving and apologizing and how important it is for us but most of all, to God. I told him that when we refuse to apologize for our actions and forgive them for theirs, we are in the same position they are in. We are all wrong. When we finished running errands, we went back home and as soon as we walked through the door, my son went straight to his sister and said "I'm sorry" and she told him she was sorry and then they hugged each other. My heart was filled with so much joy, because the atmosphere had changed in our home. It went from having that heavy feeling to feeling like Love was in the air. The enemy meant it for bad but **Aint God Good Yall.**

We all may say or do something that might hurt someone once in our lives (maybe twice), but we have to remember that Love is very powerful and in the end as long as we have Jesus we can stand against anything the enemy tries to send our way. We, being God's children, have to stand up and take back everything that the enemy has tried to steal or has stolen from us. Let's take back our peace, our joy, our self-esteem, and our Love. All of these things were given to us and no one has a right to take them away.

# I Didn't See It But God Did

Did you know that God is all seeing and all knowing? God sees things that we can't see and He knows things that we don't have a clue about. I'm so thankful that I have a God that watches over me. I remember one night everyone had gone to bed. I would always put the TV on channel zero before going to sleep, just to have a little light in the room. I had been doing this for about a year but this particular night the TV came back on. So, I got the remote and put it back on zero and it came on again. This was strange to me but I put it back on zero once again. The TV came on again but this time it was very loud. I sat up in the bed to try to figure out what was wrong with it and when I sat up I smelled gas. So, I jumped up and ran to the kitchen to find my stove on. The whole house was filled with gas and I had a space heater on in my bedroom. I know it was God watching over my family and I know it was ONLY GOD who kept turning the tv on because after that night it never came on again when I put it on channel zero. We put our trust in a lot of things but there is only one that you can trust and that's God Almighty. God watches over us even when we are not able to watch over ourselves. He sees things we can't see and that is why we should pray and ask God to watch over us and protect us from dangers seen and unseen. God is all knowing and we need Him more than we think we do.

# + Notes ‒

GOD

LOVES

YOU

# Old Habits

D o you sometimes feel like you know exactly what to do, you are excited about it, get it done and then all of a sudden, **Doubt Creeps In**. You start to question yourself. Did I do it right? Was I supposed to do that? Maybe I should do it a little different? When you start something that God tells you to do, the enemy will not let you do it without a fight. He will put all kinds of thoughts in your mind and do everything possible to make you quit. He will use people (some that are closest to you) to hinder you. When these people get in the way, please remember this:

*Ephesians 6:12-13 (NKJV)*
For we do not wrestle against flesh and blood, but against principalities, against powers, against the rulers of the darkness of this age, against spiritual hosts of wickedness in the heavenly places. Therefore take up the whole armor of God, that you may be able to withstand in the evil day, and having done all, to stand.

Please do not hate your brothers and sisters and please do not judge them. God's word says that none of us are in a position to judge.

*Matthew 7: 1- 2 (NKJV)*
Judge not, that you be not judged. For with what
judgment you judge, you will be judged; and with the
measure you use, it will be measured back to you.

When God gives us our instructions, He will give us everything we need to complete the task. He will give us strength and joy when obstacles get in our way. He will give us wisdom, knowledge and understanding to know what to do and what to say, and He will give us direction, so that we will know which way to go.

We have to keep our mind on Christ, because any little distraction can cause us to lose focus. When we lose focus, we are sure to either stop doing what we are supposed to be doing or we will start procrastinating.

Being about God's business can be overwhelming sometimes. We try so hard to make sure that what we are doing is perfect. We try so hard until we start to get stressed and that's when we start to doubt ourselves. (God knows He is not dealing with perfect people) When we start stressing and doubting, we tend to run back to old habits. These old habits seem to calm us and make us comfortable. They always make us feel like we are in control. Now, that's how they make us feel, but that's not what is really happening. What is happening is that our old habits are really controlling us.

We will find ourselves making up excuses for why the old habits are **no big deal** (I can handle it). If it wasn't a big deal and we could handle it, we would have quit a long time ago and we would not keep picking it back up every time a little turbulence comes our way.

Have you noticed that none of our old habits are healthy for us? Some of our habits are smoking, drinking, lying, stealing or running with the wrong crowd. Running back to these old habits can be very dangerous. First of all, when we are dealing with an old habit, that habit always comes before God. We put more time in with that habit, than we do with God.

Take me for instance, I had an unusual habit, I ate flour (self rising). Strange, yes. I wanted to eat it in the morning, evening and night (all day long). The more I tried to give it up, the more I wanted it. After I took a look at the situation, I realized that I was seeking after the flour more than I was seeking after God. I put in a little time with God, but not as much time as I put in with the flour. I told myself and my husband that I could handle it. I would just eat a little at a time and everything would be all right. After I ate a little here, I wanted to eat a little more and a little more. Eventually, my little more's added up to a lot. I realized that I could not handle it and I wanted it more than I wanted God's word. (DANGEROUS)

When we put something or someone before God, that is very dangerous.

*Exodus 34:14 (NKJV)*
For you shall worship no other god: for the Lord,
whose name is Jealous, is a jealous God.

*Deuteronomy 6:15 (NKJV)*
For the Lord your God is a jealous God among you,
lest the anger of the Lord your God be aroused against
you and destroy you from the face of the earth.

Not only is it dangerous because it was acting as my little god, but it was dangerous to my health. I ate so much of the flour that I didn't eat real food. My body was not getting all of the nutrients that it needed, so I felt sick all the time. (But I was happy)

We have to fight this battle with the strength of the Lord. He is the only one who can help us overcome these strongholds. I know we think we can handle it, but without God this will be a long-term war between us and those old habits. Rest assure that those old habits will not let us go without a fight. They <u>need</u> something to hold on to, but we have **Someone** to hold on to and His strength is perfect.

# Repeat (Do It Again)

Have you ever failed a test in school? Failing a test in school is a little different from failing a test in life situations. Sometimes the teacher will let you do a make-up test and other times you have to accept that grade and pray that you do better the next time. Well, it's different when it comes to life situations. If you fail the test, you will have a make-up test until you pass.

I had this habit of stressing about everything. I stressed if we couldn't pay a bill but most of all, I stressed over my children. I would stress about every little detail when it came to my children, but then it happened. It was time to take my test. My youngest daughter was getting ready to go to Kindergarten and this would be her first time riding the bus. I was very nervous about it because they could never tell me the right bus number that she would be riding. When we got to the bus stop that morning, we found out the right bus number for her. So, I changed the number on her tag that she had to wear to school for the first few weeks. That evening, I was waiting for her at the bus stop and when the bus came, my daughter was NOT on it. (I bet you can guess what I did next. Yes I panicked) I drove back to my house and called the school and they told me they didn't know what bus they put her on. (I felt the Holy Spirit telling me to calm down and pray; Honestly I didn't do it) I screamed and I cried because at that time there were a lot of children being kidnapped. So, I started flagging down buses to find my child and the first bus that I stopped, she was on it. I ran on the bus to get her and she looked at me and said "mommy, why are you crying?" She was just as happy as she could be and didn't have a care in the world. I knew I had failed that test, so I said to God "I know I failed that test, but would you please not let me take that test again". Well two days later, I had to take the test again. I was at the bus stop to pick up my oldest daughter and she didn't get off the bus. I almost panicked, but this time I stayed calmed and I prayed. As soon as I finished praying, I saw my daughter coming up the hill with one of her friends from the neighborhood. She told me that the bus was full and she couldn't get a seat so her friend got off the bus and walked home with her. I passed that test and I haven't taken that one again.

When we are faced with situations that can cause us to panic, it is so important for us to stay calm and pray. God is not taken by surprise during our circumstances, He just wants us to trust Him. We have to learn to put everything in God's hand. We have to be more like the little children. They don't worry about anything because they already know that mom and dad are going to take care of them. We should know that our Father is going to take care of us. Old habits are sometimes hard to break but the habit of stressing was broke that day.

What are you stressing about? Are you holding on to bad habits? Tell God about it.

# ✛ Notes ⚊

# Be Patient

B EING PATIENT IS sometimes so hard to do, especially when you need or want something badly, but being impatient can be costly. If you are an impatient person, you can move too fast and it can cost you money and/or time.

The road to patience can be long and frustrating, but it is necessary. We are impatient for so many reasons, but one of the main reasons is because we keep our eyes on people/things and not on God. We are always looking at what people have or where they are and then we try hard to get there. What they have and where they are is not what God wants us to have or where He wants us to be. If we rush to get to a certain place in our lives, we will miss out on some very important lessons. These lessons are very important because they will help us deal with issues in our everyday lives and they will help us to grow in Christ. To become a patient person, we have to go through some difficult times. It is a must that we go through trials and tribulations, because they bring about patience.

### Romans 5:3-4 (NKJV)

And not only that, but we also glory in tribulations, knowing that tribulations produces perseverance; and perseverance, character and character; hope.

### James 1:2-4 (NKJV)

My brethren, count it all joy when you fall into various trials; knowing that the testing of your faith produces patience. But let patience have its perfect work, that you may be perfect and complete, lacking nothing.

When we are impatient, we are very easily irritated; we get angry about any little thing and we always seem to hurt the people we love the most. There is nothing that we have to be anxious for, because God has already said that He will supply all of our needs according to His riches in glory by Christ Jesus. (Philippians 4:19 NKJV))

When we are going through our tests and trials, we have to have plenty of patience. God does not work in our time, He works in His time. Even though God's time seems like an eternity to us; it is always right on time. When we pray and ask God to work in our lives and our situations, He already knows what we need and when we need it. He just wants us to trust Him and believe that what He says is true. God says He will never leave us nor forsake us, so therefore; we have nothing to fear. God has always been in the blessing business. There is nothing too big or too small for God to handle but there is that one little thing you have to remember: God does things in His own time.

## When It Doesn't Seem Fair

How long have you been doing all that you know to do and you are still in the same place you seemed to have been for years?

*Galatians 6:9 (NKJV)*
And let us not grow weary while doing good: for in
due season we shall reap, if we do not lose heart.

Hold on! A change is on the way. It may seem like everything is at a stand still, but if you look back and think about where you started from and where you are now, you will see that you have come a long way. You have experienced some things and you have learned some valuable lessons. We don't recognize Spiritual things because we are always looking for material things. We think we are blessed when we have material things like money, cars, houses etc. , but that is not true. We are truly blessed when we receive spiritual growth, wisdom, knowledge, understanding of God's word and the Love and peace of God. When the money is gone, the car has broken down and the house is deteriorating, what do you have left? But when we are spiritually blessed it will last forever. If we are patient, everything will work out for our good, because we are patiently waiting on God and God knows exactly what we need and when we need it.

# Mr. and Mrs. Impatient

My husband and I were so very impatient. We did things without consulting God and we lost money in the process. Our house had no living room nor dining room furniture, so we went out to get furniture because we wanted to start inviting friends over. Oh, did I mention that we were very immature when it came to our finances? We got the furniture and our house was looking goooood. A few months into making payments, we got behind. Well, one day we had company over and guess who else decided to drop by. You guessed it. That was so embarrassing. We eventually had to give the furniture back and we lost our money. I'm glad to say that we have grown concerning our finances and we do have furniture. We had to learn to be patient.

# ✛ Notes ━

HE'LL KEEP YOU

IN

PERFECT PEACE

JUST

KEEP YOUR MIND

STAYED ON HIM

# Believe In Yourself

HAVE YOU EVER gone through some things and you couldn't figure out why you went through the things that you did? You are not alone. Many of us have gone through situations as children and growing up. There are so many trying to figure out why they were molested, raped, and abused, etc. We often ask the question "why me"? I've asked that question so many times. I remember sitting in my pastor's office and I said those words but what he said to me next changed everything. He said "why not you"? I am not trying to down-play these things, but all things work together for our good.

*Romans 8:28-30 (NKJV)*
And we know that all things work together for good to those who love God, to those who are the called according to His purpose. For whom He foreknew, He also predestined to be conformed to the image of His Son, that He might be the firstborn among many brethren. Moreover whom He predestined, these He also called; whom He called, these He also justified: and whom He justified, these He also glorified.

God knows everything that we have gone through or are going through, and what we have gone through and are going through is not for us. When we go through things, it is so important for us to keep our eyes on God because He always uses our situations to strengthen us because He will put someone in our path that has gone through the same thing that we have gone through. The only way we can be able to minister to the person God puts in our path is if we stand on God's word and endure until the end. God wants to use us so that others will come to know Him in His power because of the story that we have to tell about where He has brought us from and how he saved and delivered us. When we recognize the power that God has given us, we will be able to stand with our heads held high knowing that the battle has already been won and we don't have anything to fear (not one thing).

## Who Can Stop Me Now?

There is only one person who can stop you from being successful and that is Y O U. No matter what no one else says or does, you are the only one who can stop you. Those negative things that were told to us in the past can keep us in bondage if we let them, but we have to realize that God did not tell us those things. The things that God says and the things that people say are totally different.

If someone told you that you will never amount to anything, they lied.

*1Peter: 2:9a (NKJV)*
But you are a chosen generation, a royal priesthood,
a holy nation, His own special people;

If someone told you that no one will ever love you, they lied.

*John 3:16 (NKJV)*
For God so loved the world that He gave His
only begotten Son, that whoever believes in Him
should not perish but have everlasting life.

Negative things that people say are weapons that the enemy tries to use against us to keep us from prospering. People speak negative things against others for so many reasons but the main two are because they just like to hurt others or they have been hurt so many times in the past that all they know how to do is hurt others. (Hurt people hurt people)

*Matthew 5:11-12 (NKJV)*
Blessed are you when they revile and persecute you, and say
all kinds of evil against you falsely for My sake. Rejoice and
be exceedingly glad, for great is your reward in heaven, for
so they persecuted the prophets who were before you.

Whatever the reason is we have to remember that: Words may hurt but they won't kill you and what doesn't kill you will make you stronger.

*Isaiah 54:17 (NKJV)*
**No weapon** formed against you shall prosper; and every
tongue which rises against you in judgment you shall

condemn. This is the heritage of the servants of the LORD, and their righteousness is from me, says the LORD

## Why Do We Choose To Believe The Lies?

We choose to believe the lies because we don't know what the truth is and we choose to believe the lies because that's what we think of ourselves. We always put ourselves down and beat ourselves up about the things that have happened a long time ago or maybe within the last couple of days. No matter when it happened, we have to believe that God truly loves us. We can not wait on others to believe in us. We have to believe in ourselves in order to stay in the race. The enemy has all kinds of tricks up his sleeves to keep us from believing the truth. The enemy is and always will be a liar.

We often put ourselves down because just in case we don't succeed, we don't have to be ashamed. It is easier to go with the negative and hope for the positive. Success does not work like that. Success is being positive about everything that you say and do. We do not have to give in to those negative thoughts and feelings because they are not from God. God's words, His love and His promises are true. If we can't depend on nothing or no one else, we can always depend on God. He has never let us down and He has always been there, even when we have turned our backs on Him. So, just remember that everything that was told to us that does not line up with God's word is a **LIE**.

**Remember:**

**A Lie does not have power; it's your belief in the lie that gives it power. So, choose to believe in Christ because He has all power in His hand and then choose to believe in yourself because He has given you power to do all things through Him. Nothing is Impossible through Christ! What are some of the things that were told to you in the past? Write them down and give them to God.**

# Believe In You

People say what they want to say

And you hold back your tears

Deep down inside you believe what they say

Because you have so many fears

Fear of all the things you've done wrong

All the mistakes that you made

Trying to keep the secrets

So that no one will know of your pain

You say enough to answer the questions

But not enough to be read

You're afraid of what they might say

If they knew about the thoughts in your head

> Believe in yourself
> No matter what it looks like
> No one can stop you but you

> Believe in yourself
> And keep your head up
> You have to believe in you

Does this sound like you? If so, Start Believing in You

# ✤ Notes ⚊

_____

_____

_____

_____

_____

_____

_____

_____

_____

_____

_____

_____

_____

_____

_____

_____

_____

_____

_____

_____

_____

_____

_____

_____

_____

_____

WEEPING MAY

ENDURE

FOR A NIGHT

BUT

JOY COMES IN

THE

MORNING

# The Victory

E very thing that is spoken about in this book has so much to do with the way we speak: Our attitudes, Tithing, Our past, Our prayer life, Forgiving, Excuses we make and Our trials. Each topic can bring out the negative, if we don't keep our eyes on Christ. These things can cause us to say things that are hurtful and speaking evil is not of God.

*Psalm 34:13 (NKJV)*
Keep your tongue from evil, and your lips from speaking deceit.

*Psalm 52:2 (NKJV)*
Your tongue devises destruction; Like a
sharp razor, working deceitfully.

*2 Corinthians 5:17 (NKJV)*
Therefore, if anyone is in Christ, he is a new creation; old
things have passed away; behold, all things have become new.

We have **VICTORY** in Christ Jesus therefore there is nothing that can hold us back from those things that God has in store for us.

*Romans 8:38-39 (NKJV)*
For I am persuaded that neither death, nor life, nor
angels, nor principalities, nor powers, nor things present,
nor things to come, nor height, nor depth, nor any
other created thing, shall be able to separate us from
the love of God, which is in Christ Jesus our Lord.

God truly loves us and there is nothing or no one that can separate us from Him. And we have known and believed the love that God has for us. God is love; and He who abides in love abides in God, and God in him. (1 John 4:16 NKJV)) We don't have to worry about what lies ahead of us because our God already knows what's before us and He has already given us the **VICTORY**.

For the Lord your God is the one who goes with you to fight for you against your enemies to give you victory. With God we will gain the victory, and He will trample down our enemies. Psalm 108:13 (NIV)

There is nothing that can come our way that we are not more than able to handle.

**VICTORY** - Achievement of mastery or success in a struggle or endeavor.

## We Have The Victory

Now may our Lord Jesus Christ Himself, and our God and Father, who has loved us and given us everlasting consolation and good hope by grace, comfort your hearts and establish you in every good word and work. 2 Thessalonians 2:16-17 NKJV

AMEN

# Afterword

I HAVE LEARNED SO much while writing this book. One scripture will cover every area of your life (Just imagine what the whole bible will do for us). God is so amazing. It is so important for us to read His word daily. I ask you to read James 5:16 and meditate on it. This very scripture can be the scripture that will make the (positive) difference in your life. And I pray that you will find a secret place where only you and God will dwell as you come to know Him in spirit and in truth.

*Psalm 91:1 (NKJV)*
He who dwells in the secret place of the Most High
Shall abide under the shadow of the Almighty

One more thing: If you can't find anyone to encourage you: **Encourage Yourself.**

**\*There may be a long list of people that don't believe**

in you; just make sure your name is not on that list.
**Believe in Yourself**

I love you all with the love of Christ.

Thank you so much.

# ✦ What's On Your Mind? ⚊

_____

_____

_____

_____

_____

_____

_____

_____

_____

_____

_____

_____

_____

_____

_____

_____

_____

_____

_____

_____

_____

_____

_____

_____

BUT THE GOD OF
ALL GRACE,

WHO HATH CALLED
US UNTO HIS

ETERNAL GLORY BY
CHRIST JESUS,

AFTER THAT YE HAVE
SUFFERED A

WHILE, MAKE YOU
PERFECT, STABLISH,

STRENGTHEN, SETTLE YOU

1 PETER 5:10

# God's Promises

## God's Promises concerning Forgiveness:

But I say unto, Love your enemies, bless them that curse
you, do good to them that hate you, and pray for them
which despitefully use you and persecute you; That ye
may be the children of your Father which is in heaven:
for He maketh His sun to rise on the evil and on the
good, and sendeth rain on the just and on the unjust
**Matthew 5:44-45 KJV**

And when ye stand praying, forgive, if ye have ought against
any: that you Father also which is in heaven may forgive
you your trespasses. But if ye do not forgive, neither will
your Father which is in heaven forgive your trespasses.
**Mark 11:25-26 KJV**

For if ye forgive men their trespasses, your
heavenly Father will also forgive you.
**Matthew 6:14 KJV**

Therefore if thine enemy is hungry, feed
him; if he thirst, give him drink.
**Romans: 12:20 KJV**

But love ye your enemies, and do good, and lend, hoping for
nothing again; and your reward shall be great, and ye shall be
the children of the Highest: for He is kind unto the thankful
and the evil. Be ye therefore merciful, as your Father also is
merciful. Judge not, and ye shall not be judged: condemn not,
and ye shall not be condemned: forgive, and ye shall be forgiven.
**Luke 6: 35-38 KJV**

## God's Promises concerning praying:

Ask and it shall be given you; seek, and ye shall find; knock, and it
shall be opened unto you: For every one that asketh receiveth; and
he that seeketh findeth; and to him that knocketh it shall be opened.
**Matthew 7:7-8 KJV**

And all things, whatsoever ye shall ask in
prayer, believing, ye shall receive.
**Matthew 21:22 KJV**

And it shall come to pass, that before they call, I will
answer; and while they are yet speaking, I will hear.
**Isaiah 65:24 KJV**

Whatsoever ye shall ask the Father in my name, He will
give it you. Hitherto have ye asked nothing in my name:
ask, and ye shall receive, that your joy may be full.
**John 16:23-24 KJV**

Confess your faults one to another, and pray one for
another, that ye may be healed. The effectual fervent
prayer of a righteous man availeth much.
**James 5:16 KJV**

If ye abide in me, and my words abide in you, ye shall
ask what ye will, and it shall be done unto you.
**John 15:7 KJV**

If ye then, being evil, know how to give good gifts unto
your children, how much more shall your Father which
is in heaven give good things to them that ask Him?
**Matthew 7:11 KJV**

And whatsoever we ask, we receive of Him,
because we keep His commandments, and do
those things that are pleasing in His sight.
**1 John 3:22 KJV**

# God's Promises concerning Repentance:

The time is fulfilled, and the kingdom of God is
at hand: repent ye, and believe the gospel.
**Mark 1:15 KJV**

Repent ye therefore, and be converted, that your sins
may be blotted out, when the times of refreshing
shall come from the presence of the Lord.
**Acts 3:19 KJV**

But if the wicked will turn from all his sins that he
hath committed, and keep all my statutes, and do
that which is lawful and right, he shall surely live,
he shall not die. All his transgressions that he hath
committed, they shall not be mentioned unto him: in
his righteousness that he hath done he shall live.
**Ezekiel 18:21-22 KJV**

For I am not come to call the righteous, but sinners to repentance.
**Matthew 9:13 KJV**

# God's Promises concerning Joy

They that sow in tears shall reap in joy. He that goeth forth
and weepeth, bearing precious seed, shall doubtless come
again with rejoicing, bringing his sheaves with him.
**Psalm 126:5-6 KJV**

These things have I spoken unto you, that my joy might
remain in you, and that your joy might be full.
**John 15:11 KJV**

Therefore the redeemed of the Lord shall return, and
come with singing unto Zion; and everlasting joy shall
be upon their head: they shall obtain gladness and
joy; and sorrow and mourning shall flee away.
**Isaiah 51:11 KJV**

Whom having not seen, ye love; in whom, though now ye see Him
not, yet believing, ye rejoice with joy unspeakable and full of glory.
**1 Peter 1:8 KJV**

I will see you again, and your heart shall rejoice,
and your joy no man taketh from you.
**John 16:22 KJV**

For ye shall go out with joy, and be led forth with peace: the
mountains and the hills shall break forth before you into
singing, and all the trees of the field shall clap their hands.
**Isaiah 55:12 KJV**

# God's Promises concerning Fear:

Be not afraid of sudden fear, neither of the desolation of
the wicked, when it cometh. For the Lord shall be thy
confidence, and shall keep thy foot from being taken.
**Proverbs 3:25-26 KJV**

For God hath not given us the spirit of fear; but of
power, and of love, and of a sound mind.
**2 Timothy1:7 KJV**

So that we may boldly say, The Lord is my helper,
and I will not fear what man shall do unto me.
**Hebrews 13:6 KJV**

He shall cover thee with His feathers, and under His wings
shalt thou trust: His truth shall be thy shield and buckler.
Thou shalt not be afraid for the terror by night; nor for the
arrow that flieth by day; Nor for the pestilence that walketh in
darkness; nor for the destruction that wasteth at noonday.
**Psalm 91:4-6 KJV**

Yea, though I walk through the valley of the shadow
of death, I will fear no evil: for thou art with me; thy
rod and thy staff they comfort me. Thou preparest a
table before me in the presence of mine enemies: thou
anointest my head with oil; my cup runneth over.
**Psalm 23:4-5 KJV**

# God's Promises concerning Guilt:

If we confess our sins, He is faithful and just to forgive us
our sins, and to cleanse us from all unrighteousness.
**1 John 1:9 KJV**

For the Lord your God is gracious and merciful, and will
not turn away His face from you, if ye return unto Him.
**2 Chronicles 30:9 KJV**

As for as the east is from the west, so far hath
He removed our transgressions from us.
**Psalm 103:12 KJV**

Therefore if any man be in Christ, he is a new creature: old things are passed away; behold, all things are become new.
**2 Corinthians 5:17 KJV**

For I will forgive their iniquity, and I will remember their sin no more.
**Jeremiah 31:34 KJV**

But if we walk in the light, as He is in the light, we have fellowship one with another, and the blood of Jesus Christ His Son cleanseth us from all sin.
**1 John 1:7 KJV**

# God's Promises concerning Guidance

For this God is our God for ever and ever: He will be our guide even unto death
**Psalm 48:14 KJV**

A man's heart deviseth his way: but the Lord directeth his steps.
**Proverbs 16:9 KJV**

The steps of a good man are ordered by the Lord: and he delighteth in his way.
**Psalm 37:23 KJV**

In all thy ways acknowledge Him, and He shall direct thy paths.
**Proverbs 3:6 KJV**

# ✦ Notes ━

_____

_____

_____

_____

_____

_____

_____

_____

_____

_____

_____

_____

_____

_____

_____

_____

_____

_____

_____

_____

_____

_____